# TWILA PARIS

PIANO · VOCAL · GUITAR

*true north*

ISBN 0-634-01237-1

HAL•LEONARD®
CORPORATION

7777 W. BLUEMOUND RD. P.O. BOX 13819 MILWAUKEE, WI 53213

Visit Hal Leonard Online at
**www.halleonard.com**

# RUN TO YOU

Words and Music by
TWILA PARIS

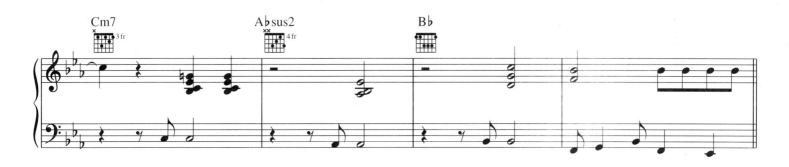

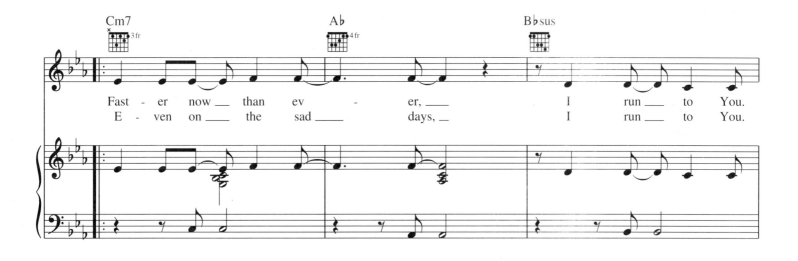

Fast - er now __ than ev - __ er, __ I run __ to You.
E - ven on __ the sad __ days, __ I run __ to You.

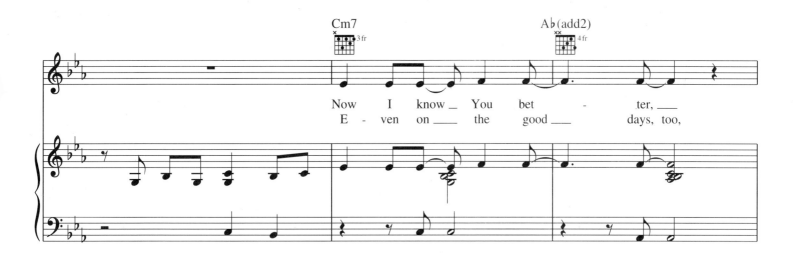

Now I know __ You bet - ter, __
E - ven on __ the good __ days, too,

# TRUE NORTH

Words and Music by
TWILA PARIS

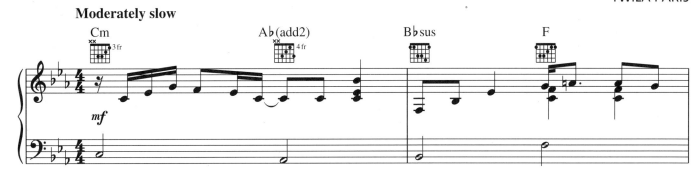

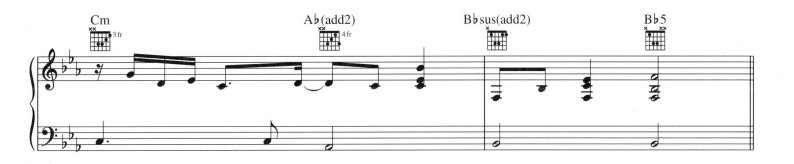

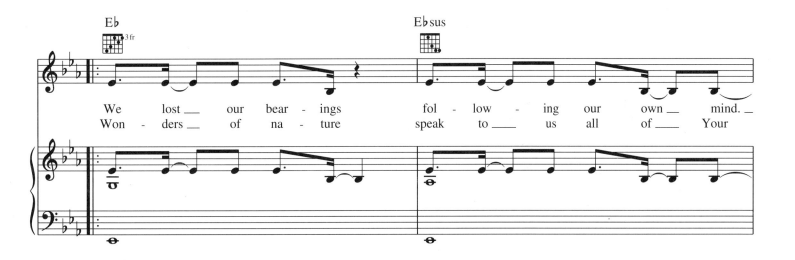

We lost our bear-ings fol-low-ing our own mind.
Won-ders of na-ture speak to us all of Your

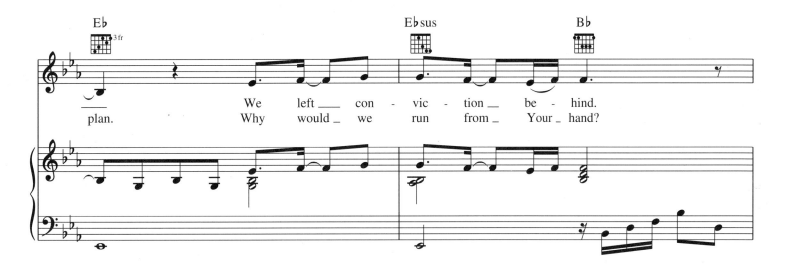

plan. We left con-vic-tion be-hind.
Why would we run from Your hand?

# NO CONFIDENCE

Words and Music by
TWILA PARIS

# DELIGHT MY HEART

Words and Music by
TWILA PARIS

So man-y plans, ___ so man-y dreams, ___
All that I want, ___ think that I need, ___

live _ in - side _ me. _____ I will de - light _

in You. _

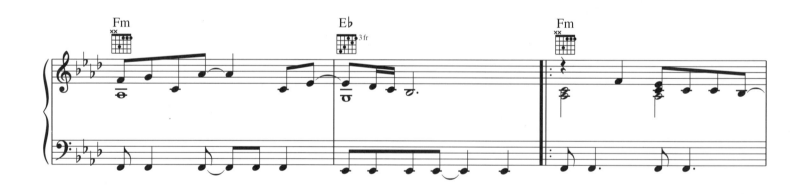

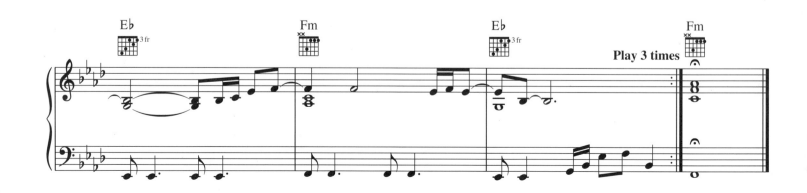

# WISDOM

Words and Music by
TWILA PARIS

**Moderately slow groove**

I see a mul - ti - tude __ of peo - ple,
There is a mo - ment of __ de - ci - sion,

30

# I CHOOSE GRACE

Words and Music by
TWILA PARIS

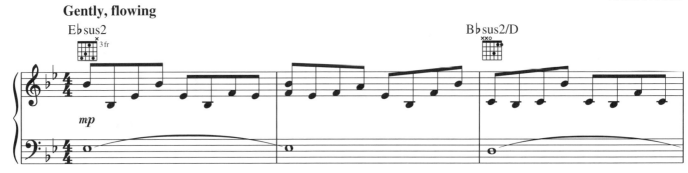

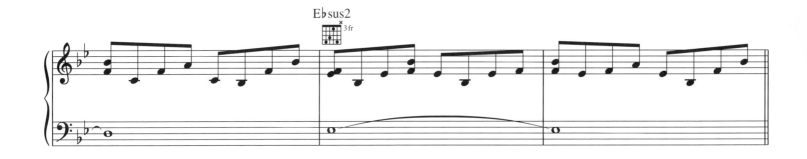

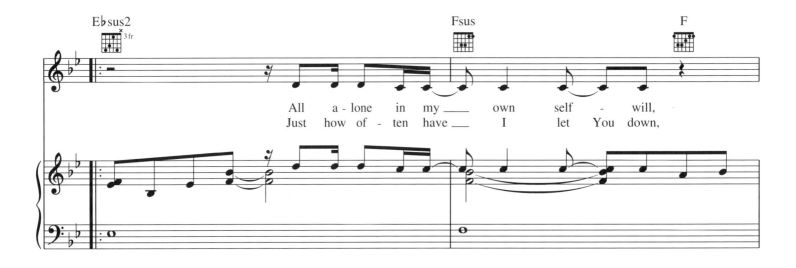

All a-lone in my ___ own self - will,
Just how of - ten have ___ I let You down,

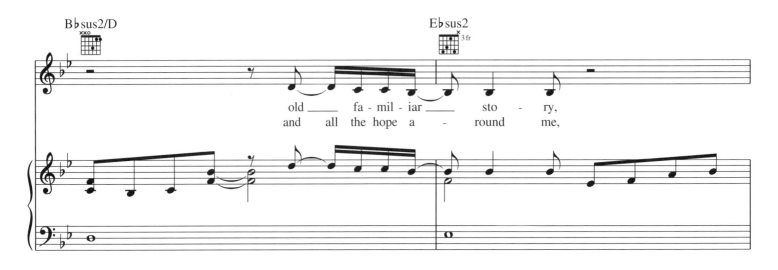

old ___ fa - mil - iar ___ sto - ry,
and all the hope a - round me,

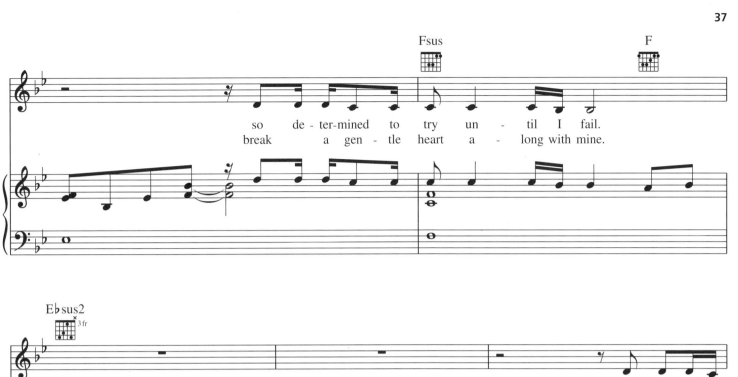

so de-ter-mined to try un-til I fail.
break a gen-tle heart a - long with mine.

You've been wait-ing
You keep hold-ing

as I learn _ a-gain,                    strain - ing to the pres-sure,
out Your arms _ a-gain,                 just ___ the way You found me,

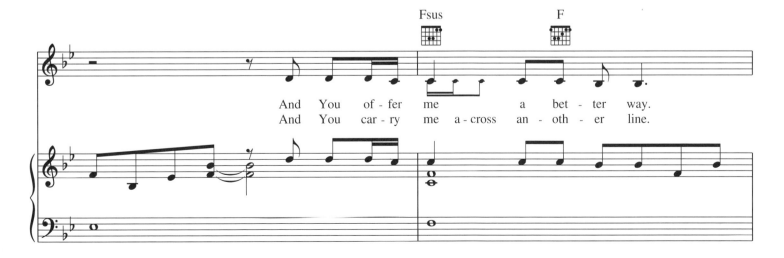

And You of-fer me a bet-ter way.
And You car-ry me a-cross an - oth - er line.

# COULD YOU BELIEVE

Words and Music by
TWILA PARIS

*Original key: G# minor. This edition has been transposed down one half-step to be more playable.*

Could you _____ be - lieve? _____

# DAUGHTER OF GRACE

Words and Music by
TWILA PARIS

**She** went down _ so low, _ thought she'd nev-
**She** spent half _ her life _ work-ing hard _

-er, ev-er find _ the sur- face _ a- gain.
_ to be some-one _ you had _ to _ ad- mire,

Went so far a- stray,
met the ex- pec- ta-

52

53

# ONCE IN A LIFETIME

Words and Music by
TWILA PARIS

# WONDERING OUT LOUD

Words and Music by
TWILA PARIS

Look-ing  through _ this  win - dow  pane _____
Then a - gain ___ an - oth - er  day, _____

at  the  world _ near - by, _____
dif - f'rent  point _ of  view. ___

# WHEN YOU SPEAK TO ME

Words and Music by
TWILA PARIS

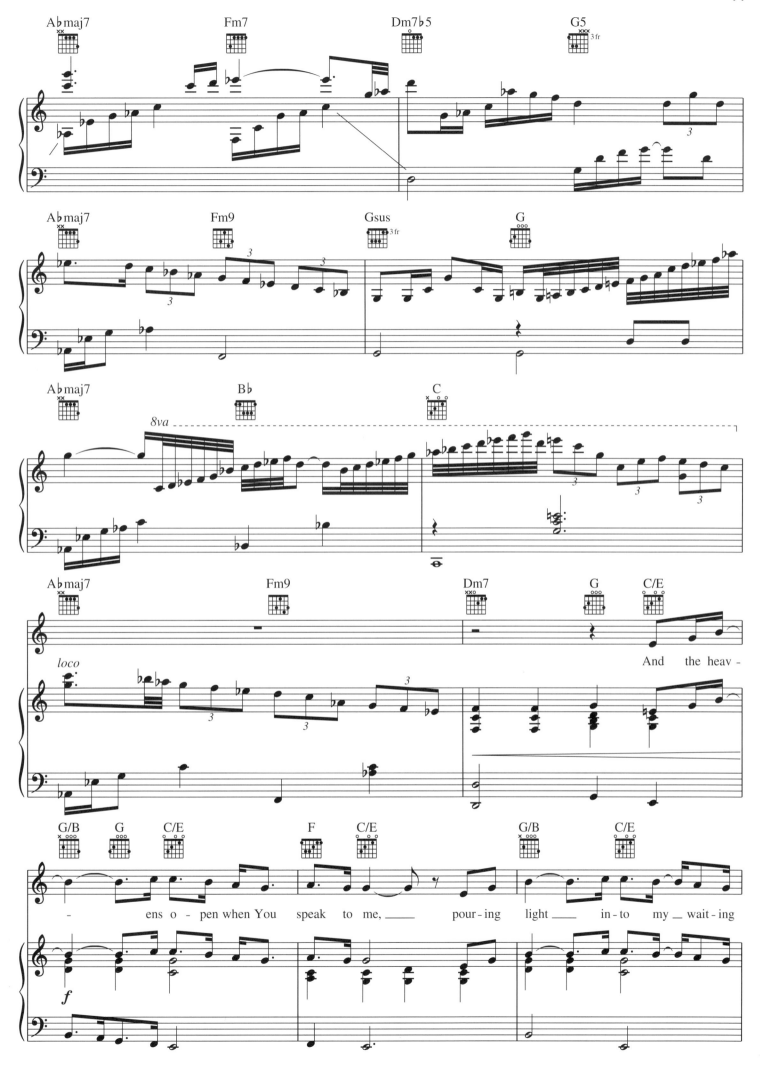